New Year, New Magic

# New Year, New Magic

Matthew Petchinsky

# New Year, New Magic: Manifesting Your Best Year Yet
By: Matthew Petchinsky

**Introduction**: *Start Fresh, Start Strong*

The New Year is more than just the turn of a calendar page; it is a powerful moment of renewal, brimming with potential and possibility. It's a time when the collective energy of billions around the globe is focused on transformation, making it the perfect moment to realign your life and manifest your deepest desires. But what does it mean to truly "start fresh"? How can you harness this moment to not only set resolutions but to create a magical, transformative year that aligns with your higher purpose?

This introduction will guide you into understanding the true essence of manifestation, the extraordinary power of setting clear intentions, and the profound impact of aligning your goals with the flow of universal energy. Together, we will explore how to craft rituals and practices that go beyond the ordinary, creating a spiritual and practical framework to ensure this year becomes a turning point in your life.

**The Power of a New Year**

The New Year has long been regarded as a symbolic reset—a moment to reflect on what was and to dream of what could be. Across cultures and traditions, this time has been marked by celebrations of renewal and transformation, from the setting of New Year's resolutions to rituals for good luck and prosperity.

But why is this moment so powerful? The answer lies in intention and focus. The energy of a new beginning is amplified when you consciously participate in it, and the New Year offers a natural opportunity to do just that. When you take time to reflect on your past, identify what no longer serves you, and set a clear vision for your future, you tap into the universal flow of energy that supports growth and transformation.

This energy is not just symbolic; it is tangible. By consciously harnessing the power of this time, you can align yourself with the natural cycles of change and renewal, turning your hopes and dreams into reality. But this requires more than wishful thinking. It requires action, intention, and the commitment to create a plan that bridges your inner world with the outer.

**How Manifestation Works**

Manifestation is the process of turning your thoughts and desires into reality by aligning your energy, beliefs, and actions with your goals. It is not about simply wishing for things to happen but about intentionally creating the conditions for your dreams to unfold.

At its core, manifestation operates on the principle that energy follows thought. What you focus on grows. When you set a clear intention and back it with belief, emotion, and aligned action, you activate a powerful force within yourself and the universe. This process involves three key components:

1. **Clarity**: Know what you want. Vague or conflicting desires dilute your energy. Instead, set specific and meaningful goals that resonate with your true self.
2. **Belief**: Trust that what you desire is possible and that you are worthy of receiving it. Belief is the foundation that supports your manifestation practice.
3. **Action**: Take inspired steps toward your goals. Manifestation requires you to be a co-creator, actively participating in bringing your desires to life.

By weaving these elements into your New Year rituals, you can turn the abstract concept of manifestation into a practical tool for transformation.

### The Importance of Setting Intentions

Intentions are the driving force behind any meaningful change. Unlike resolutions, which often focus on rigid outcomes, intentions are about aligning your energy with your deeper desires. They act as a compass, guiding your thoughts, actions, and decisions toward what truly matters to you.

Setting intentions at the start of the year is especially powerful because it creates a foundation for everything that follows. It shifts your focus from what you lack to what you want to cultivate, empowering you to move forward with clarity and purpose. Intentions also provide a framework for your manifestation practice, helping you stay anchored even when challenges arise.

As you set your intentions, consider these steps:

- **Reflect on the Past Year**: What lessons did you learn? What are you ready to release?
- **Dream Boldly**: What do you truly desire in the year ahead? What lights you up?
- **Stay Grounded**: Align your intentions with your values and long-term goals.

**Rituals and Practices for a Transformative Year**

Rituals are a powerful way to ground your intentions and connect with the universal energy of renewal. They create space for reflection, celebration, and action, blending the spiritual with the practical. By incorporating rituals into your New Year's practice, you can amplify your manifestation efforts and set the tone for a year of growth and abundance.

Here are a few rituals to consider:

- **Cleansing Ritual**: Clear your space of old energy through smudging, decluttering, or an energetic reset. Let go of anything that no longer serves you.
- **Journaling**: Write down your intentions for the year, along with affirmations and gratitude for what you've already achieved.
- **Vision Board Creation**: Create a visual representation of your goals to keep you inspired and focused.
- **New Year's Meditation**: Spend time in quiet reflection, visualizing the year ahead and connecting with your higher self.

These rituals are more than symbolic. They create an intentional container for your energy, helping you stay focused and aligned with your goals.

**The Year Ahead**

The New Year is a blank canvas, waiting for you to paint it with the colors of your dreams and desires. This book will guide you step-by-step through the process of manifesting a magical and meaningful year. From setting intentions and building daily rituals to aligning your goals with universal energy, you'll learn how to turn the promise of a fresh start into lasting change.

As you embark on this journey, remember that transformation is not a one-time event but an ongoing process. Each day offers an opportunity to realign, recalibrate, and recommit to your vision. By starting fresh and starting strong, you can create a year that not only meets your expectations but surpasses them in every way. Let's make this the year you manifest your best life.

### Chapter 1: Manifestation Foundations

*Discover the principles of manifestation and how to harness your energy to align with your goals for the New Year.*

### What Is Manifestation?

Manifestation is the art and science of turning thoughts, desires, and intentions into tangible reality. At its core, it is a process of aligning your energy, beliefs, and actions with the goals you want to achieve. Contrary to the common misconception that manifestation is simply "wishful thinking," it is a deliberate practice rooted in focus, intention, and action.

The principles of manifestation are grounded in universal laws, such as the Law of Attraction, which states that like attracts like. This means the energy you project—through your thoughts, feelings, and actions—will attract experiences that match it. For example, if you consistently think positively about achieving a goal, take aligned actions, and believe in your ability to succeed, you are more likely to create the circumstances that lead to that success.

**The Key Principles of Manifestation**

To successfully manifest your goals for the New Year, it is essential to understand and apply the following foundational principles:

**1. Clarity of Desire**

Manifestation begins with knowing exactly what you want. Vagueness or indecision weakens your ability to focus your energy.

- Why it matters: Clear goals create a clear path. The universe—and your subconscious—responds to precision.
- How to apply it: Take time to write down your desires in specific, measurable terms. For example, instead of saying, "I want to be healthier," specify, "I want to lose 10 pounds by June by exercising three times a week and eating a balanced diet."

**2. Energy Alignment**

Your thoughts, emotions, and actions must be in harmony with what you want to manifest. If you want abundance but constantly dwell on lack, you are sending mixed signals to the universe.

- **Why it matters**: Energy alignment ensures that you attract circumstances and opportunities that support your goals.
- **How to apply it:** Practice positive thinking, gratitude, and visualization daily to keep your energy aligned with your desires.

### 3. Belief and Self-Worth

Manifestation is fueled by your belief in its possibility and your own worthiness to receive it. Doubt creates energetic blocks that hinder progress.

- **Why it matters:** Without belief, your efforts will lack the conviction needed to manifest effectively.
- **How to apply it:** Use affirmations, self-reflection, and inner work to build confidence and dissolve limiting beliefs.

### 4. Inspired Action

Manifestation is not passive; it requires active participation. Taking steps toward your goals signals your commitment to the universe and creates momentum.

- **Why it matters:** Action bridges the gap between intention and reality.
- **How to apply it:** Break down your goals into manageable steps and take consistent, meaningful actions every day.

### 5. Patience and Trust

Manifestation does not always happen on your timeline. Trust that the universe is working behind the scenes to align the right circumstances and opportunities for you.

- **Why it matters:** Impatience and doubt can create resistance that delays your manifestations.
- **How to apply it:** Focus on the journey rather than obsessing over the outcome. Celebrate small wins along the way.

## How to Harness Your Energy for the New Year

Harnessing your energy is about becoming an active participant in shaping your life. The New Year is an ideal time to do this because it marks a natural shift in energy—a collective sense of hope, renewal, and possibility. Here's how you can channel this momentum into your manifestation practice:

### 1. Reflect on the Past Year

Before setting goals for the New Year, take time to assess the year that has passed. Reflect on what worked, what didn't, and what you've learned.

- **Questions to ask yourself:**
    - **What were my biggest accomplishments and how did they make me feel?**
    - **What challenges did I face, and what lessons did they teach me?**
    - **What patterns or habits am I ready to leave behind?**

### 2. Set Intentions for the Year Ahead

Intentions are the foundation of manifestation. They serve as a roadmap for where you want to direct your energy and focus.

- **How to set intentions:**
    - **Start with a quiet moment of meditation or journaling.**
    - **Write down your goals in the present tense, as if they are already happening (e.g., "I am thriving in my career and earning $80,000 this year").**

    ◦ **Align your intentions with your values to ensure they are meaningful and sustainable.**

### 3. Create an Energetic Anchor

An energetic anchor is a physical or symbolic representation of your goals that helps you stay focused and motivated.

- **Examples of anchors:**
    - ◦ **A vision board filled with images and affirmations that represent your desires.**
    - ◦ **A crystal or talisman infused with your intentions.**
    - ◦ **A journal where you track your progress and express gratitude.**

### 4. Practice Daily Alignment

Manifestation is an ongoing process that requires consistent effort to stay in energetic alignment with your goals.

- **Daily practices to align your energy:**
    - ◦ **Morning affirmations to set a positive tone for the day.**
    - ◦ **Visualization exercises where you vividly imagine yourself achieving your goals.**
    - ◦ **Gratitude journaling to focus on abundance rather than lack.**

**Overcoming Common Manifestation Blocks**

Manifestation challenges often arise when your energy is out of alignment or when subconscious fears and doubts interfere. Here are some common blocks and how to address them:

**Block: Limiting Beliefs**

- **What it is:** Deep-seated thoughts that tell you you're not good enough, smart enough, or deserving of your goals.
- **How to overcome it:** Challenge these beliefs through affirmations and inner work. Replace "I can't" with "I am capable."

**Block: Fear of Failure**

- **What it is:** The fear that you will not succeed, which prevents you from even trying.
- **How to overcome it:** Reframe failure as a learning opportunity. Every step, even a misstep, moves you closer to your goals.

**Block: Impatience**

- **What it is:** The urge to see results immediately, which creates frustration and doubt.
- **How to overcome it:** Trust the process. Focus on the progress you're making, not the speed at which it's happening.

**Setting the Stage for the Year Ahead**

As you embark on your manifestation journey this New Year, remember that success lies in your ability to align your energy, take inspired action, and trust in the process. Manifestation is not just a one-time practice but a way of life—a continuous cycle of dreaming, creating, and evolving.

By mastering these foundational principles, you are laying the groundwork for a transformative year, one where your goals are not just aspirations but tangible realities. Let this be the year you fully step into your power and create the life you've always envisioned.

## Chapter 2: The Power of Intentions

*Learn how to set meaningful and achievable New Year's resolutions that stick by connecting them to your values and desires.*

### What Are Intentions and Why Are They Powerful?

Intentions are the foundation of meaningful action. Unlike resolutions, which often focus solely on achieving specific outcomes, intentions reflect a deeper alignment with your values, emotions, and aspirations. They go beyond surface-level goals and anchor you to the "why" behind your actions.

For example, a resolution might be, "I will lose 20 pounds this year." An intention, on the other hand, could be, "I will nurture my body and cultivate health through nourishing foods and joyful movement." The latter connects to your core values and creates a sense of purpose, making it easier to stay committed.

Intentions are powerful because they:

1. **Clarify Your Focus**: They serve as a compass, helping you prioritize what truly matters.
2. **Create Emotional Resonance**: They tap into your feelings, which motivates sustained action.
3. **Invite Flexibility**: Unlike rigid resolutions, intentions allow for growth and adaptation as your journey unfolds.

Setting intentions for the New Year enables you to craft a vision for your life that resonates on a deep, personal level, creating a foundation for lasting change.

## The Difference Between Resolutions and Intentions

| Resolutions | Intentions |
| --- | --- |
| Outcome-focused | Value-driven |
| Often rigid and unrealistic | Flexible and adaptable |
| Rooted in external validation | Rooted in personal growth |
| Focus on what you lack | Focus on what you want to cultivate |

By shifting your mindset from resolutions to intentions, you replace pressure with purpose, making it easier to stick to your goals.

**The Psychology of Setting Intentions**

Intentions work because they align with the brain's natural processes for change. Here's why:

1. **Emotional Anchoring**: Intentions create emotional connections to your goals, which strengthens your motivation.
2. **Neuroplasticity**: Repeatedly focusing on your intentions rewires your brain, making new behaviors and habits easier to adopt.
3. **Reward System Activation**: Achieving small steps aligned with your intentions releases dopamine, reinforcing positive behaviors.

When you set intentions that resonate with your desires and values, you engage both your conscious mind and subconscious beliefs, creating a powerful synergy for success.

## How to Set Meaningful Intentions for the New Year

### 1. Reflect on Your Values

Your values are the guiding principles of your life. When your intentions align with your values, they become deeply meaningful and sustainable.

- **Exercise**: Write down your top 5 values. These might include health, family, creativity, financial security, or adventure.
- **Ask Yourself**: How can I live in greater alignment with these values this year?

For example: If "creativity" is a core value, your intention might be, "I will embrace creativity daily by writing, painting, or exploring new ideas."

### 2. Define Your Desires

Intentions should reflect what you truly want, not what you think you should want. This distinction is crucial because externally imposed goals often lack the intrinsic motivation needed for follow-through.

- **Exercise**: Sit in a quiet space and ask yourself:
    - What do I truly desire in the coming year?
    - How do I want to feel as I move through my life?
    - What would success look like for me?

Write down your answers without judgment. These reflections will form the basis of your intentions.

### 3. Make Your Intentions Clear and Specific

While intentions are broader than resolutions, they should still be clear enough to provide direction. Avoid vague statements like, "I want to be happier." Instead, reframe it as, "I intend to cultivate joy by practicing gratitude and spending time with loved ones."

## 4. Use Positive Language

Focus on what you want to cultivate, not what you want to avoid. For example, instead of saying, "I don't want to feel stressed," say, "I intend to create calm by prioritizing self-care and setting boundaries."

## 5. Connect Intentions to Actions

Intentions without action are just dreams. Break down your intentions into actionable steps that you can integrate into your daily routine.

- **Example**:
  - **Intention**: "I will prioritize my health this year."
  - **Actions**:
    - Schedule 30 minutes of exercise 5 days a week.
    - Replace processed snacks with whole foods.
    - Drink 8 glasses of water daily.

**Creating New Year's Intentions That Stick**

**Step 1: Start with Gratitude**

Gratitude shifts your mindset from lack to abundance, creating a positive foundation for setting intentions.

- **Exercise**: Write down three things you're grateful for from the past year. Reflect on how these experiences can inspire your intentions for the year ahead.

**Step 2: Visualize Your Ideal Year**

Visualization helps you connect emotionally with your goals, making them more tangible and achievable.

- **Exercise**: Close your eyes and imagine it's the end of the year. Picture your ideal life. What have you accomplished? How do you feel? What does your day-to-day look like? Write down the key elements of this vision.

**Step 3: Write Your Intentions**

Use the insights from the previous exercises to craft 3–5 meaningful intentions.

- **Format Example**:
  - "I intend to..."
  - "I will cultivate..."
  - "I choose to prioritize..."

**Step 4: Create Reminders**

Keep your intentions visible to reinforce them daily.

- Place them on sticky notes around your home.
- Add them to your journal or planner.
- Use them as affirmations during meditation.

### Examples of Intentions for the New Year

- "I intend to nurture my body by moving joyfully and eating nourishing foods."
- "I will prioritize my mental health by setting boundaries and practicing mindfulness."
- "I intend to cultivate deeper connections with my loved ones by being present and attentive."
- "I will create abundance by pursuing opportunities that align with my passions and talents."
- "I choose to embrace creativity by dedicating time to my art and exploring new ideas."

### Overcoming Challenges in Staying Committed

Even with meaningful intentions, challenges can arise. Here's how to stay on track:

### 1. Revisit Your Why

When motivation wanes, reconnect with the values and desires that inspired your intentions.

### 2. Practice Self-Compassion

Progress isn't always linear. If you stumble, avoid self-criticism and focus on getting back on track.

### 3. Adjust as Needed

Intentions are not set in stone. As life evolves, your priorities may shift. Be open to revising your intentions to reflect your current needs.

### The Ripple Effect of Intentions

Setting powerful intentions doesn't just transform your life; it influences the energy you bring into the world. When you act with purpose and alignment, you inspire those around you to do the same. As you move through the year, let your intentions guide you toward a life that feels meaningful, joyful, and authentically yours.

This New Year, don't just set resolutions. Set intentions that resonate with your heart and soul—and watch as they transform your life from the inside out.

## Chapter 3: Creating a Vision Board for Success

*Step-by-step guidance on designing a vision board that brings clarity and focus to your dreams.*

### What Is a Vision Board and Why Is It Powerful?

A vision board is a visual representation of your goals, dreams, and aspirations. It is a physical or digital collage of images, words, and symbols that reflect what you want to manifest in your life. By focusing on your vision board regularly, you create a clear mental picture of your desired outcomes, which helps align your thoughts, emotions, and actions with your goals.

The power of a vision board lies in:

1. **Clarity**: It helps you define your goals with precision.
2. **Focus**: It keeps your aspirations front and center, making it easier to stay motivated.
3. **Energy Alignment**: By visualizing your dreams daily, you align your energy with your desires, activating the Law of Attraction.
4. **Emotional Engagement**: Seeing images that resonate with your dreams triggers positive emotions, reinforcing your commitment to your goals.

### The Science Behind Vision Boards

The effectiveness of vision boards is supported by neuroscience and psychology:

- **Visualization and the Brain**: When you visualize your goals, your brain activates the same neural pathways as it would if you were physically achieving them. This primes your mind to recognize and seize opportunities that align with your vision.
- **Reticular Activating System (RAS)**: Your brain's RAS filters the information you encounter daily, prioritizing what aligns with your focus. A vision board programs your RAS to notice opportunities and resources related to your goals.
- **Positive Reinforcement**: Regularly viewing a vision board triggers the brain's reward system, reinforcing motivation and persistence.

**Step-by-Step Guide to Creating Your Vision Board**
**Step 1: Clarify Your Goals**
Before you start creating your vision board, take time to reflect on what you truly want. A vision board is most effective when it focuses on specific, meaningful goals.

- **Exercise**: Write down your goals for different areas of your life, such as:
    - **Career**: What do you want to achieve professionally?
    - **Health**: How do you envision your physical and mental well-being?
    - **Relationships**: What kind of connections do you want to nurture?
    - **Finances**: What are your financial goals for the year?
    - **Personal Growth**: What skills, habits, or experiences do you want to develop?
    - **Lifestyle**: What kind of environment or daily routine do you dream of?

Prioritize the goals that resonate most deeply with your values and desires.

### Step 2: Gather Supplies

The materials you choose will depend on whether you're creating a physical or digital vision board.

- **For a Physical Vision Board**:
    - A poster board, corkboard, or large piece of cardboard.
    - Magazines, newspapers, or printed images from the internet.
    - Scissors, glue sticks, or pins.
    - Markers, stickers, or decorative elements for personalization.
- **For a Digital Vision Board**:
    - Use tools like Canva, Pinterest, or graphic design software.
    - Collect images and quotes online that resonate with your goals.

## Step 3: Choose Images and Words

Select visuals and text that evoke strong emotions and clearly represent your goals. Each element should inspire you and remind you of what you're working toward.

- **Tips for Selecting Images**:
    - Choose pictures that closely align with your goals. For example, if you want to travel, include photos of specific destinations.
    - Pick images that make you feel excited, inspired, and motivated.
    - Include personal photos if they represent a meaningful aspect of your vision.
- **Incorporating Words**:
    - Add affirmations, quotes, or keywords that reinforce your goals (e.g., "Abundance," "Health," "Success," "Joy").
    - Use words that evoke strong emotional connections to your dreams.

## Step 4: Arrange Your Vision Board

The way you organize your vision board can enhance its effectiveness. Here are a few strategies:

- **Sectioned Layout**: Divide your board into categories (e.g., career, health, relationships) and group related images together.
- **Freeform Layout**: Place images and words wherever they feel most intuitive or inspiring.
- **Timeline Layout**: Arrange your goals in a progression, starting with short-term goals and moving toward long-term aspirations.

**Pro Tip**: Leave some blank space on your board to symbolize openness to unexpected blessings and opportunities.

### Step 5: Personalize Your Board

Your vision board should feel uniquely yours. Add creative touches that make it personal and meaningful.

- Use colors, stickers, or drawings that represent your personality.
- Include symbols or items that hold special significance to you (e.g., a feather for freedom, a sun for positivity).

### Step 6: Place Your Vision Board Strategically

To maximize the impact of your vision board, place it somewhere you'll see it regularly.

- **Examples**:
  - On a wall in your bedroom or office.
  - As the background of your phone or computer (for digital boards).
  - In a journal or planner that you use daily.

### Step 7: Engage with Your Vision Board Daily

Creating a vision board is just the beginning. The real magic happens when you actively engage with it.

- Spend a few minutes each day visualizing yourself living the life depicted on your board.
- Recite affirmations aloud while looking at your board to reinforce your intentions.
- Reflect on your progress and update your board as needed to keep it aligned with your evolving goals.

**Common Mistakes to Avoid**

While creating a vision board is simple, there are a few pitfalls to watch out for:

1. **Overloading Your Board**: Too many images and words can dilute your focus. Stick to your most meaningful goals.
2. **Lack of Specificity**: Vague visuals or phrases won't evoke the same emotional and mental clarity as specific ones.
3. **Neglecting Your Board**: A vision board is a tool, not a one-time project. Engage with it consistently to keep your energy aligned.

**Success Stories: How Vision Boards Work**

Countless individuals have achieved extraordinary results by using vision boards. From athletes visualizing victories to entrepreneurs manifesting business success, these stories demonstrate the transformative power of this practice.

- Oprah Winfrey credits vision boards for helping her manifest career milestones.
- Jim Carrey famously wrote himself a $10 million check for "acting services rendered," visualized his success daily, and eventually achieved his goal with a movie deal.

These examples show that when paired with intention and action, a vision board can become a powerful catalyst for change.

**The Final Step: Believe and Act**

A vision board is not a magical solution; it's a tool that amplifies your focus and determination. To make your dreams a reality, you must combine belief with inspired action.

- Use your vision board to stay motivated when challenges arise.
- Trust that the universe is aligning opportunities in your favor.

- Take consistent steps toward your goals, knowing that each effort brings you closer to your vision.

By following this step-by-step process, your vision board will become a dynamic and inspiring representation of your dreams, guiding you toward a successful and fulfilling New Year.

## Chapter 4: Daily Rituals for Positive Momentum

*Explore easy-to-implement rituals to start each day with purpose and gratitude.*

### Why Daily Rituals Matter

Rituals are powerful tools that structure your day, infuse it with meaning, and align your energy with your intentions. Unlike habits, which are often automatic and unconscious, rituals are deliberate actions performed with purpose and mindfulness. Starting your day with intentional rituals creates a ripple effect, setting a positive tone that carries into everything you do.

Daily rituals help:

1. **Anchor Your Focus**: By beginning your day with clarity, you reduce stress and increase productivity.
2. **Strengthen Your Mindset**: Positive rituals condition your mind to see opportunities rather than obstacles.
3. **Align Your Energy**: Rituals connect you with your higher purpose, keeping you grounded and motivated.
4. **Cultivate Gratitude**: Starting the day with gratitude rewires your brain to focus on abundance and joy.

**The Elements of a Powerful Morning Ritual**

A successful morning ritual doesn't have to be long or complicated. It should include actions that:

- **Align Your Mind**: Practices like journaling or affirmations that create mental clarity.
- **Nourish Your Body**: Activities like stretching, hydration, or a healthy breakfast that energize your physical self.
- **Inspire Your Spirit**: Meditations or visualizations that connect you to your goals and purpose.

The following sections provide easy-to-implement daily rituals to help you start your day with positive momentum.

### Ritual 1: Morning Gratitude Practice

Gratitude is one of the most transformative practices for shifting your mindset from lack to abundance. When you start your day by focusing on what you're grateful for, you train your brain to look for the positive in every situation.

### How to Practice Gratitude in the Morning:

1. **Write It Down**: Keep a journal by your bed and list 3–5 things you're grateful for each morning. Be specific (e.g., "I'm grateful for the warmth of my coffee" rather than "I'm grateful for my life").
2. **Say It Aloud**: Speak your gratitude aloud to reinforce it emotionally.
3. **Feel It**: Take a moment to truly feel the gratitude in your heart. This emotional connection amplifies the impact of the practice.

### Example:

- "I am grateful for the quiet morning that allows me to reflect."
- "I am thankful for my family's health and happiness."
- "I appreciate the opportunities today will bring."

**Ritual 2: Hydration and Mindful Nourishment**
Starting your day with hydration and nourishing your body supports physical and mental clarity.
**How to Hydrate and Nourish Mindfully:**

1. **Drink Water First**: Before your coffee or breakfast, drink a glass of water with lemon to rehydrate and kickstart your metabolism.
2. **Eat Intentionally**: Choose a healthy breakfast that fuels your body, such as oatmeal, fruit, or a smoothie.
3. **Be Present**: Eat without distractions. Focus on the taste, texture, and nourishment your food provides.

**Bonus Tip**: As you drink water or eat, set an intention for the day (e.g., "May this food give me energy to stay focused and productive").

### Ritual 3: Morning Movement

Physical activity stimulates your body, clears your mind, and boosts endorphins, making it an ideal way to start the day.

**Ideas for Morning Movement:**

1. **Stretching or Yoga**: Spend 5–10 minutes stretching or practicing yoga to release tension and energize your body.
2. **Walk Outside**: A quick walk in nature can calm your mind and connect you with the present moment.
3. **Cardio or Strength Training**: If you prefer a more vigorous start, a 20-minute workout can invigorate your entire system.

**Pro Tip**: Pair movement with an affirmation or mantra to amplify its impact (e.g., "I am strong, capable, and ready for today").

### Ritual 4: Visualization for Success

Visualization is a mental practice where you vividly imagine yourself achieving your goals. It activates your subconscious mind, strengthens belief in your ability to succeed, and aligns your actions with your desired outcomes.

**How to Practice Visualization:**

1. **Find a Quiet Space**: Sit somewhere comfortable and free of distractions.
2. **Set a Timer**: Spend 5–10 minutes visualizing your day or long-term goals.
3. **Create a Mental Movie**: Imagine yourself successfully completing tasks or achieving milestones. Focus on the details—what you see, hear, and feel.
4. **Feel the Emotions**: Connect with the excitement, joy, or pride you'll feel when your vision becomes reality.

**Example**: Visualize yourself confidently delivering a presentation, acing an interview, or enjoying time with loved ones.

### Ritual 5: Affirmations for Positivity

Affirmations are positive statements that help reprogram your mind to focus on your strengths and potential. They counteract self-doubt and negative thinking, reinforcing confidence and motivation.

**How to Use Affirmations:**

1. **Write Personalized Affirmations**: Tailor affirmations to your goals and challenges (e.g., "I am worthy of success" or "I approach today with courage and clarity").
2. **Speak Them Aloud**: Say your affirmations in front of a mirror to enhance their impact.
3. **Repeat Daily**: Consistency is key to embedding affirmations in your subconscious mind.

**Examples:**

- "I am capable of achieving my dreams."
- "I attract opportunities that align with my purpose."
- "I face today's challenges with confidence and ease."

**Ritual 6: Setting Daily Intentions**

Intentions guide your actions and keep you aligned with your long-term goals. By setting an intention each morning, you ensure that your day is purposeful and focused.

**How to Set Daily Intentions:**

1. **Reflect on Your Priorities**: Ask yourself, "What is the most important thing I want to accomplish today?"
2. **Phrase Your Intention Positively**: Use language that inspires action (e.g., "I intend to communicate clearly in my meetings today").
3. **Write It Down**: Keep your intention visible throughout the day by writing it in your planner or on a sticky note.

**Examples**:

- "I intend to approach today with patience and kindness."
- "I will stay focused on completing my top three tasks."
- "I intend to bring creativity and joy to my work."

### Ritual 7: Morning Meditation for Clarity

Meditation is a powerful way to calm your mind, center your energy, and prepare for the day ahead.

**How to Meditate in the Morning:**

1. **Choose a Quiet Spot**: Sit comfortably in a place where you won't be interrupted.
2. **Set a Timer**: Start with 5–10 minutes and gradually increase as you become more comfortable.
3. **Focus on Your Breath**: Take slow, deep breaths, inhaling for a count of four, holding for four, and exhaling for four.
4. **Use a Mantra**: Repeat a calming phrase like "I am at peace" or "I am open to today's opportunities."
5. **Visualize Calm**: Imagine a wave of light washing over you, clearing stress and filling you with positive energy.

### Tips for Building a Consistent Morning Ritual

1. **Start Small**: Incorporate one or two rituals at a time to avoid feeling overwhelmed.
2. **Be Flexible**: Adapt your rituals to suit your schedule and needs. Even a five-minute practice can make a difference.
3. **Make It Enjoyable**: Choose rituals that you look forward to, turning them into moments of self-care.
4. **Track Your Progress**: Use a journal or planner to record how your rituals impact your mood, energy, and productivity.

### The Ripple Effect of Morning Rituals

Starting your day with purpose and gratitude doesn't just benefit you; it influences the way you interact with others and handle challenges throughout the day. When you take time to nurture your mind, body, and spirit each morning, you create a solid foundation for positive momentum that carries into everything you do.

Let your morning rituals be a sacred space where you connect with yourself, align with your goals, and set the tone for a successful and fulfilling day.

## Chapter 5: Letting Go of Last Year's Baggage

*Learn practical techniques for releasing negative energy, old patterns, and limiting beliefs that hold you back.*

### Why Letting Go Is Essential for Growth

The start of a new year is an invitation to leave behind what no longer serves you. Carrying the emotional weight of past experiences, negative energy, or limiting beliefs into a new chapter can prevent you from fully embracing the opportunities ahead. Letting go doesn't mean forgetting or invalidating the past—it means releasing its grip on your present and future.

By shedding last year's baggage, you create space for growth, clarity, and abundance. This process involves acknowledging what you've been holding onto, understanding its impact, and actively choosing to release it. When you let go, you free yourself to move forward with renewed energy and purpose.

### Signs You're Carrying Emotional Baggage

Before you can release baggage, it's essential to recognize it. Emotional baggage often manifests as:

- **Resentment or Anger**: Lingering frustration over past events or relationships.
- **Self-Doubt**: A fear of failure or belief that you're not good enough.
- **Repeating Patterns**: Finding yourself stuck in similar situations, like toxic relationships or unfulfilling jobs.
- **Procrastination or Avoidance**: Delaying important actions due to unresolved fears or anxieties.
- **Physical Symptoms**: Stress, fatigue, or tension resulting from emotional weight.

If any of these resonate with you, it's time to take proactive steps to release and reset.

**Step 1: Acknowledge and Identify What Needs to Be Released**

The first step in letting go is recognizing the baggage you're carrying. This could be old patterns, relationships, limiting beliefs, or past mistakes.

**Reflection Exercise:**

1. **Write It Down**: Take a blank piece of paper or journal and list the things you feel are holding you back. These might include:
   - Specific events or situations from last year.
   - Negative self-talk or beliefs.
   - Toxic relationships or unresolved conflicts.
   - Regrets or feelings of failure.

2. **Ask Yourself**:
   - Why am I holding onto this?
   - How is this affecting my life today?
   - What would my life look like if I let this go?

Acknowledging your baggage is a powerful act of self-awareness and the first step toward release.

### Step 2: Release Negative Energy

Negative energy accumulates when emotions like anger, sadness, or fear remain unresolved. Releasing this energy clears your mental and emotional space for positivity and growth.

**Techniques for Releasing Negative Energy:**

1. **Journaling**:
   - Write a letter to yourself or the person/situation that caused the pain. Pour out your emotions without holding back. End the letter with words of forgiveness or closure, even if you never send it.
   - Burn or shred the letter as a symbolic act of release.

2. **Physical Release**:
   - Engage in activities that help you physically release tension, such as punching a pillow, dancing, or going for a run.
   - Try shaking therapy: Stand and gently shake your body from head to toe, imagining negative energy falling away.

3. **Energy Cleansing Rituals**:
   - Use sage, palo santo, or incense to cleanse your space and yourself. As you smudge, visualize the smoke carrying away negativity.
   - Take a salt bath. Epsom salts help detoxify your body and soothe your energy. Add essential oils like lavender for extra relaxation.

4. **Meditation**:
   - Sit in a quiet space, close your eyes, and imagine a warm light washing over you, dissolving negativity and filling you with peace.

**Step 3: Break Free from Old Patterns**

Old habits and patterns often keep us stuck in cycles of frustration or failure. Breaking these patterns requires conscious effort and a willingness to create new ones.

**Steps to Break Patterns:**

1. **Identify Triggers**:
   - Reflect on the situations, emotions, or environments that lead to unhelpful behaviors.
2. **Reframe Your Mindset**:
   - Instead of focusing on what went wrong, shift your perspective to what you can learn. For example, if a past relationship failed, think about how it helped you grow or what qualities you now seek in a partner.
3. **Set Boundaries**:
   - Protect your energy by setting clear boundaries with people or situations that trigger old patterns. Learn to say no and prioritize your well-being.
4. **Replace Habits**:
   - Swap unhealthy habits with positive ones. For instance, replace mindless scrolling with reading or practicing a hobby.
5. **Celebrate Small Wins**:
   - Breaking patterns takes time. Acknowledge and reward yourself for progress, no matter how small.

**Step 4: Release Limiting Beliefs**

Limiting beliefs are the inner narratives that convince you of your shortcomings or create self-imposed boundaries. Common limiting beliefs include:

- "I'm not good enough."
- "Success isn't for people like me."
- "I always fail, so why try?"

**How to Overcome Limiting Beliefs:**

1. **Challenge the Belief**:
   - Write down your limiting beliefs and ask, "Is this really true? What evidence do I have to support or refute this?"
2. **Reframe the Belief**:
   - Replace negative statements with empowering ones. For example:
     - Limiting Belief: "I'm not smart enough to start my own business."
     - Reframed Belief: "I have the ability to learn and grow, and I'm capable of creating success."
3. **Use Affirmations**:
   - Create affirmations that counter your limiting beliefs and repeat them daily (e.g., "I am deserving of love and success.").
4. **Surround Yourself with Positivity**:
   - Engage with people, books, and media that inspire and uplift you.

### Step 5: Forgive and Move Forward

Forgiveness is one of the most liberating acts of letting go. It doesn't mean condoning harmful behavior—it means freeing yourself from the emotional chains of resentment.

### How to Practice Forgiveness:

1. **Forgive Yourself**:
   - Reflect on mistakes or regrets and remind yourself that you did the best you could with the knowledge and resources you had at the time.
   - Use affirmations like, "I forgive myself and allow myself to move forward."

2. **Forgive Others**:
   - Acknowledge the pain caused by others, but choose to release its hold on you.
   - Visualize the person surrounded by light and say, "I release you and the power this situation has over me."

3. **Symbolic Acts**:
   - Write down the name of someone you need to forgive and what you are forgiving them for. Burn or tear the paper to symbolize release.

### Step 6: Create Space for Renewal

Once you've released old baggage, it's time to fill the space with positive energy and intentions.

**Steps to Create Renewal:**

1. **Cleanse Your Environment**:
   - Declutter your living space to create a fresh, uplifting atmosphere.
2. **Embrace New Experiences**:
   - Try something new, like a hobby, travel, or connecting with new people.
3. **Visualize Your Future**:
   - Spend time imagining the life you want to create. Use this vision as motivation to keep moving forward.

### Final Thoughts

Letting go of last year's baggage is not an instant process—it's a journey of self-awareness, intention, and action. By acknowledging what no longer serves you and releasing it with purpose, you create room for growth, joy, and fulfillment.

As you let go of the past, remind yourself that every ending is a new beginning. With the weight lifted, you can step into the New Year with clarity, confidence, and the freedom to embrace all the possibilities ahead.

## Chapter 6: Financial Manifestation for the New Year

*Master the art of attracting wealth and abundance through affirmations, money rituals, and a prosperity mindset.*

### What Is Financial Manifestation?

Financial manifestation is the process of aligning your thoughts, emotions, beliefs, and actions with the energy of abundance to attract wealth and financial opportunities. It goes beyond wishful thinking; it's about intentionally creating a mindset and environment that invite prosperity. By understanding and applying the principles of financial manifestation, you can transform your relationship with money, eliminate limiting beliefs about wealth, and open the door to greater financial freedom.

### The Principles of Financial Manifestation

1. **Abundance Is a Mindset**: True wealth begins in the mind. To attract money, you must believe that abundance is available to you and that you are deserving of it.
2. **Energy Follows Focus**: Whatever you focus on grows. If you dwell on lack or fear of financial hardship, you perpetuate scarcity. Focus on gratitude, growth, and opportunities to attract abundance.
3. **Money Is Energy**: Money is not just a physical resource; it is energy that flows in and out of your life. Aligning your energy with financial abundance makes it easier to attract wealth.

**Step 1: Reframe Your Money Beliefs**

Many people carry subconscious limiting beliefs about money, such as:


- "Money is the root of all evil."
- "I'll never have enough."
- "Rich people are greedy."
These beliefs create energetic blocks that repel wealth.

**How to Reframe Limiting Money Beliefs:**

1. **Identify Your Money Stories**:
    - Write down any negative beliefs or feelings you have about money. Ask yourself where these beliefs originated (e.g., childhood, societal norms).

2. **Challenge Your Beliefs**:
    - For each limiting belief, write down evidence that contradicts it. For example, if you believe "I'll never have enough," list moments when money came to you unexpectedly or when you were financially secure.

3. **Create Empowering Beliefs**:
    - Replace negative thoughts with positive affirmations, such as:
        - "Money flows to me easily and abundantly."
        - "I am worthy of wealth and success."
        - "I attract financial opportunities effortlessly."

4. **Visualize Abundance**:
    - Close your eyes and imagine living in financial freedom. Feel the emotions of joy, gratitude, and security as if it's already your reality.

**Step 2: Cultivate a Prosperity Mindset**

A prosperity mindset is about focusing on possibilities, opportunities, and gratitude rather than fear or scarcity.

**Practical Ways to Develop a Prosperity Mindset:**

1. **Practice Gratitude:**
   - Each day, write down three things you're grateful for about your current financial situation, no matter how small. Gratitude shifts your focus from lack to abundance.

2. **Celebrate Small Wins:**
   - Acknowledge every financial success, whether it's saving $5 or landing a big client. This reinforces positive energy around money.

3. **Surround Yourself with Abundance:**
   - Spend time with people who have a healthy relationship with money and success. Engage with books, podcasts, and content that inspire financial growth.

4. **Invest in Yourself:**
   - View spending on education, skills, or wellness as an investment in your future wealth.

**Step 3: Use Affirmations to Attract Wealth**

Affirmations are powerful tools for reprogramming your subconscious mind to align with financial abundance. Repeating positive statements regularly helps you internalize new beliefs about money.

**Examples of Money Affirmations:**

- "I am open to receiving unlimited wealth."
- "I am financially free and live in abundance."
- "Every day, I attract more money and opportunities."
- "I am grateful for the wealth that flows into my life."

**How to Use Money Affirmations:**

1. Repeat affirmations daily, especially in the morning or before bed.
2. Write them in a journal to reinforce their power.
3. Say them with emotion and belief to amplify their effect.

**Step 4: Create Money Rituals**

Rituals are symbolic actions that help you focus your energy and intention on attracting financial abundance.

**Money Ritual Ideas:**

1. **Prosperity Candle Ritual**:
   - Light a green or gold candle (colors associated with wealth) and focus on your financial goals. Visualize money flowing into your life. Repeat affirmations like, "This flame burns away scarcity and attracts abundance."
2. **Abundance Check**:
   - Write yourself a "check" for the amount of money you want to manifest. Place it on your vision board or somewhere visible as a daily reminder.
3. **Money Jar Spell**:
   - Fill a jar with coins, herbs (like basil or cinnamon, which are associated with wealth), and a note describing your financial goals. Keep it on your desk or altar to symbolize growing prosperity.
4. **Wealth Bath**:
   - Take a ritual bath with Epsom salts, basil, and a few coins. As you soak, visualize financial abundance washing over you.
5. **Crystal Magic**:
   - Carry or meditate with crystals like citrine, pyrite, or green aventurine, which are believed to attract wealth and success.

**Step 5: Take Aligned Action**

Manifestation works best when combined with inspired, practical action. Once you've set your intentions and aligned your energy, take steps that move you closer to your financial goals.

**Practical Actions for Financial Success:**

1. **Create a Budget**:
   - Track your income and expenses to gain clarity about your financial situation. Allocate money toward savings, investments, and personal growth.

2. **Set Clear Financial Goals**:
   - Break down big goals into actionable steps. For example, if you want to save $10,000, calculate how much you need to save monthly or weekly.

3. **Build Multiple Income Streams**:
   - Explore opportunities like freelancing, starting a side business, or investing to diversify your income sources.

4. **Invest in Education**:
   - Take courses, attend workshops, or read books to expand your financial knowledge and skills.

5. **Give Generously**:
   - Donate to causes you care about. Generosity creates a cycle of giving and receiving, reinforcing abundance.

**Step 6: Maintain Faith and Trust**

Manifestation doesn't happen overnight. It requires patience, trust, and consistent effort. Keep the faith that the universe is working in your favor and that your financial goals are unfolding at the right time.

**Tips for Staying Committed:**

- Revisit your affirmations and visualizations daily.
- Celebrate small financial wins to stay motivated.
- Trust that challenges are temporary and part of your growth.

**Success Stories of Financial Manifestation**

1. **The Power of Visualization**: A woman who visualized earning her dream salary every day eventually landed a promotion that exceeded her financial expectations.
2. **The Magic of Generosity**: A small business owner who donated 10% of her profits saw her revenue double within a year, reinforcing her belief in abundance.
3. **Aligned Action Pays Off**: A man who combined affirmations with investing in his skills created a thriving online business that surpassed his income goals.

**The Ripple Effect of Financial Abundance**

Financial manifestation doesn't just benefit you—it empowers you to support others, pursue meaningful goals, and live a life of freedom and fulfillment. By mastering the art of attracting wealth, you create a ripple effect that inspires and uplifts those around you.

This New Year, commit to transforming your financial mindset and taking intentional steps toward abundance. With the right mindset, rituals, and actions, you can manifest a prosperous and thriving future.

## Chapter 7: Building Your Magical Year Planner

*Craft a personalized planner infused with affirmations, moon phases, and seasonal cycles to stay aligned throughout the year.*

### Why a Magical Year Planner?

A planner is more than a tool to organize your time; it's a powerful way to align your intentions, actions, and energy with your goals. A magical year planner combines the practical benefits of scheduling with spiritual elements like affirmations, moon phases, and seasonal cycles, helping you stay connected to both your daily tasks and your higher purpose.

When you build your own personalized planner, you create a sacred space for reflection, planning, and manifesting. Each page becomes a reminder of your aspirations and a guide to maintaining balance throughout the year.

### The Core Elements of a Magical Year Planner

Your magical planner should include both practical and spiritual components:

1. **Affirmations**: Daily or weekly affirmations to keep you focused and motivated.
2. **Moon Phases**: A calendar of the moon's phases to align your activities with lunar energy.
3. **Seasonal Cycles**: Sections that honor the changing seasons and their corresponding energies.
4. **Goal Setting**: Spaces to define and track your goals throughout the year.

5. **Reflection Pages**: Dedicated areas for gratitude journaling, monthly reflections, and lessons learned.
6. **Personalization**: Colors, symbols, and decorations that make the planner uniquely yours.

**Step 1: Choose Your Format**

The first step in creating your magical planner is deciding on the format that works best for you.

**Physical Planner:**

- **Pros**: Tangible, customizable, and allows for creative expression with handwriting, stickers, and drawings.
- **How to Create**: Use a blank notebook, bullet journal, or pre-printed planner that you can customize.

**Digital Planner:**

- **Pros**: Portable, easily editable, and accessible across devices.
- **How to Create**: Use apps like GoodNotes, Notion, or Canva to design and manage your planner.

### Step 2: Infuse Daily Affirmations

Affirmations are powerful tools for manifesting your intentions and reinforcing a positive mindset. Including them in your planner ensures you begin each day or week with focus and purpose.

**How to Add Affirmations:**

1. **Daily Affirmations**: Write a new affirmation at the top of each day's page (e.g., "I am capable of achieving my goals today.").

2. **Weekly Themes**: Choose an affirmation for each week that aligns with your goals (e.g., "This week, I attract opportunities that support my growth.").

3. **Creative Expression**: Use colored pens, calligraphy, or stickers to make affirmations stand out on your planner pages.

### Step 3: Incorporate Moon Phases

The moon's phases have a significant influence on energy and productivity. By aligning your planner with the lunar cycle, you can schedule activities that harness the moon's energy.

**The Moon Phases and Their Meanings:**

1. **New Moon**: A time for setting intentions and starting fresh. Add sections for goal-setting and brainstorming during this phase.
2. **Waxing Crescent**: Focus on building momentum and taking small steps toward your goals. Schedule action items here.
3. **First Quarter**: Overcome challenges and make decisions. Add a "problem-solving" section in your planner for this phase.
4. **Waxing Gibbous**: Refine and perfect your plans. Use this phase for fine-tuning tasks.
5. **Full Moon**: Celebrate achievements and reflect on progress. Include space for gratitude and celebration.
6. **Waning Gibbous**: Release what no longer serves you. Use this phase for decluttering or journaling about habits to let go of.
7. **Last Quarter**: Focus on rest and self-care. Dedicate time in your planner for relaxation and rejuvenation.
8. **Waning Crescent**: Prepare for the next cycle. Use this phase to reflect and set intentions for the upcoming New Moon.

### How to Incorporate Moon Phases in Your Planner:

- Add a small moon phase symbol to each date in your planner.
- Include a brief explanation of the phase's energy on relevant pages.

- Create dedicated pages for New Moon and Full Moon rituals.

## Step 4: Honor Seasonal Cycles

The changing seasons offer natural rhythms that influence your energy and focus. Incorporating seasonal cycles into your planner helps you align your goals with nature's flow.

**The Seasonal Energies:**

1. **Winter**: A time for reflection, planning, and setting intentions.
2. **Spring**: A season of growth, new beginnings, and action.
3. **Summer**: A period of expansion, creativity, and celebration.
4. **Autumn**: A time to harvest results, express gratitude, and let go.

**How to Add Seasonal Elements:**

- Decorate your planner with seasonal colors and symbols (e.g., snowflakes for winter, flowers for spring).
- Add prompts for seasonal reflections, such as:
    - "What am I releasing this winter?"
    - "What seeds of intention am I planting this spring?"
    - "How will I celebrate my progress this summer?"
    - "What lessons have I learned this autumn?"

## Step 5: Set Goals and Track Progress

Your magical planner should include spaces for goal setting and tracking to ensure you stay on course throughout the year.

**How to Structure Goal-Setting Sections:**

1. **Yearly Goals**: Dedicate a page at the beginning of your planner for overarching goals in areas like career, health, relationships, and personal growth.
2. **Monthly Goals**: Break down yearly goals into smaller, actionable steps.
3. **Weekly Check-Ins**: Include space to review progress and adjust plans as needed.
4. **Habit Trackers**: Create grids or charts to track daily habits like meditation, exercise, or journaling.

## Step 6: Add Reflection Pages

Reflection pages allow you to assess your journey, celebrate wins, and identify areas for improvement.

**Ideas for Reflection Pages:**

1. **Gratitude Journal**: Include a section for writing down things you're grateful for each day or week.
2. **Monthly Reflections**: Add prompts like:
   ◦ "What went well this month?"
   ◦ "What challenges did I face, and how did I overcome them?"
   ◦ "What am I looking forward to next month?"
3. **End-of-Year Reflection**: Dedicate a page to reviewing the entire year, highlighting key lessons and achievements.

**Step 7: Personalize Your Planner**

The more personal your planner feels, the more you'll want to use it. Infuse it with your unique energy and creativity.

**Ways to Personalize Your Planner:**

- Add stickers, drawings, or decorative tape.
- Use your favorite colors for headings and sections.
- Include motivational quotes or personal mantras.
- Leave blank spaces for spontaneous doodles, ideas, or notes.

**Step 8: Commit to Using Your Planner Daily**

Even the most beautifully designed planner is ineffective if it's not used consistently. Commit to spending time with your planner each day to maintain alignment with your goals.

**Tips for Daily Use:**

- Set aside 5–10 minutes each morning to review your schedule and affirmations.
- Use your planner as a reflection tool at the end of the day to assess progress and plan for tomorrow.
- Keep your planner in a visible location as a constant reminder of your intentions.

## Benefits of Your Magical Year Planner

By creating and consistently using a magical year planner, you:

1. **Stay Aligned with Your Goals**: Regularly revisiting your intentions keeps you focused and motivated.
2. **Feel Connected to Nature**: Aligning with moon phases and seasonal cycles helps you flow with natural rhythms.
3. **Cultivate Gratitude and Awareness**: Daily affirmations and reflection pages foster mindfulness and positivity.
4. **Manifest More Effectively**: The planner becomes a tangible tool for tracking and amplifying your manifestations.

## Conclusion

Building a magical year planner is an act of self-care and empowerment. It's not just about staying organized—it's about creating a sacred space that inspires you to dream, plan, and achieve. With affirmations, lunar energy, seasonal cycles, and personal touches, your planner becomes a compass guiding you through the year with clarity, purpose, and joy.

As you turn the pages each day, let your planner remind you of the infinite possibilities that await when you align your actions with your intentions. This is your year—plan it magically, and watch your dreams unfold!

## Chapter 8: Manifesting Healthy Relationships

*Dive into practices for enhancing existing relationships and attracting new, meaningful connections.*

### Why Relationships Are Central to Your Well-Being

Relationships are the foundation of human experience. They shape our sense of belonging, self-worth, and emotional health. Whether it's a romantic partner, family member, friend, or colleague, the quality of our connections profoundly impacts our overall well-being. Manifesting healthy relationships means intentionally nurturing meaningful connections while letting go of toxic dynamics that no longer serve you.

This chapter will explore practices to enhance existing relationships, attract new ones, and build a relationship with yourself that supports your growth and happiness.

### Understanding Healthy Relationships

A healthy relationship is built on mutual respect, trust, communication, and emotional support. It creates a safe space for both individuals to grow while maintaining their individuality.

### Characteristics of Healthy Relationships:

1. **Respect**: Valuing each other's boundaries, opinions, and individuality.
2. **Trust**: Consistently showing honesty and reliability.
3. **Communication**: Open and honest dialogue, with active listening.
4. **Support**: Encouraging growth and providing emotional and practical help.
5. **Balance**: Equal give-and-take, avoiding one-sided dynamics.

By focusing on these principles, you can strengthen existing relationships and manifest new ones that align with your values.

**Step 1: Cultivating Self-Love and Self-Worth**

Manifesting healthy relationships begins with your relationship with yourself. When you nurture self-love and recognize your worth, you naturally attract people who respect and value you.

**How to Build Self-Love:**

1. **Acknowledge Your Worth**: Write down your strengths, accomplishments, and qualities that make you unique. Review this list regularly.
2. **Set Boundaries**: Learn to say no to people or situations that drain your energy or disrespect your boundaries.
3. **Practice Self-Care**: Prioritize activities that nourish your mind, body, and spirit, whether it's exercise, meditation, or creative hobbies.
4. **Affirm Your Value**: Use affirmations like:
    - "I am deserving of love and respect."
    - "I am enough just as I am."
    - "I attract relationships that nurture my soul."

When you truly value yourself, you elevate the energy you bring to your relationships.

### Step 2: Enhancing Existing Relationships

Healthy relationships require ongoing effort and intention. Whether you want to strengthen a romantic partnership, deepen a friendship, or improve family dynamics, small, intentional actions can make a significant difference.

### Practical Practices for Strengthening Connections:

1. **Improve Communication:**
   - Practice active listening by giving your full attention and acknowledging the other person's feelings.
   - Use "I" statements to express yourself (e.g., "I feel..." rather than "You always...").
   - Schedule regular check-ins to discuss feelings, goals, and any issues.
2. **Show Appreciation:**
   - Regularly express gratitude for the people in your life. A simple "thank you" can strengthen bonds.
   - Write a heartfelt note or give a small token of appreciation to show you care.
3. **Spend Quality Time Together:**
   - Prioritize one-on-one time without distractions, such as phones or work.
   - Plan activities that both of you enjoy, whether it's a shared hobby, a walk, or cooking a meal together.
4. **Resolve Conflicts Mindfully:**
   - Approach disagreements with a willingness to understand rather than win.
   - Focus on solutions instead of dwelling on blame.
   - Take breaks if emotions run high, then return to the conversation with a calm mindset.

5. **Support Each Other's Growth**:
    ○ Encourage your loved ones to pursue their goals and dreams.
    ○ Celebrate their achievements, no matter how small.

### Step 3: Letting Go of Toxic Relationships

Not all relationships are meant to last forever. Letting go of toxic connections is an act of self-love that creates space for healthier relationships to enter your life.

**Signs of a Toxic Relationship:**

- Consistent lack of respect or trust.
- Manipulation, control, or emotional abuse.
- Constant negativity, criticism, or lack of support.
- Feeling drained or anxious after interactions.

**How to Release Toxic Relationships:**

1. **Acknowledge the Problem**: Be honest with yourself about how the relationship is affecting your well-being.
2. **Set Clear Boundaries**: Communicate your needs and limits, and enforce them firmly.
3. **Seek Support**: Talk to a trusted friend, family member, or therapist for guidance.
4. **Detach with Compassion**: Let go without resentment, understanding that the relationship no longer aligns with your growth.
5. **Focus on Healing**: Engage in self-care practices and give yourself time to process and heal.

## Step 4: Attracting New, Meaningful Connections

If you want to manifest new relationships, whether romantic, platonic, or professional, it's essential to align your energy with the type of people you wish to attract.

### Steps to Manifest New Relationships:

1. **Get Clear on What You Want**:
   - Write a list of qualities you value in a partner, friend, or colleague.
   - Focus on traits like kindness, honesty, and shared interests rather than superficial attributes.
2. **Visualize Your Ideal Connection**:
   - Spend a few minutes each day imagining yourself surrounded by supportive, loving relationships.
   - Picture the joy and fulfillment these connections bring into your life.
3. **Use Affirmations**:
   - "I attract relationships that align with my highest good."
   - "I am surrounded by people who uplift and inspire me."
   - "Love and meaningful connections flow into my life effortlessly."
4. **Take Inspired Action**:
   - Join groups, clubs, or events where you can meet like-minded people.
   - Be open to initiating conversations and showing genuine interest in others.

5. **Radiate Positivity**:
   - ° People are drawn to positive energy. Smile, practice kindness, and express gratitude in your interactions.

## Step 5: Building a Strong Foundation for Relationships

To maintain healthy relationships, focus on building a strong foundation of trust, respect, and mutual support.

**Practical Tips for Maintaining Healthy Relationships:**

- **Prioritize Consistency**: Show up for the people in your life regularly, not just during good times.
- **Be Vulnerable**: Share your feelings and experiences openly to deepen emotional intimacy.
- **Honor Boundaries**: Respect the other person's limits and needs without taking them personally.
- **Celebrate Milestones**: Mark special occasions and achievements to create shared memories.
- **Grow Together**: Engage in activities that foster mutual learning and growth, like attending workshops or trying new hobbies.

## Step 6: Manifesting Love in Romantic Relationships

If you're manifesting a romantic partner, focus on creating a relationship rooted in love, respect, and shared values.

### Key Practices for Romantic Manifestation:

1. **Release Past Hurts**:
   - Heal from past relationships to avoid carrying emotional baggage into new ones.
2. **Embody What You Seek**:
   - Be the kind of partner you want to attract. If you value kindness, practice it daily.
3. **Write a Love Letter to the Universe**:
   - Describe your ideal partner and relationship as if it's already in your life. Focus on the feelings and experiences you desire.
4. **Trust Divine Timing**:
   - Let go of impatience and trust that the universe will bring the right person into your life at the perfect time.

## The Role of Gratitude in Relationships

Gratitude amplifies love and connection in all relationships. When you express appreciation, you attract more to be grateful for.

### Daily Gratitude Practices for Relationships:

- Keep a journal where you list things you appreciate about the people in your life.
- Share your gratitude directly with loved ones through kind words or gestures.
- Reflect on the lessons and growth you've gained from every relationship, even challenging ones.

### Final Thoughts

Manifesting healthy relationships is about intention, effort, and alignment. By cultivating self-love, nurturing existing connections, releasing toxic dynamics, and attracting meaningful new relationships, you can create a life filled with love, support, and joy.

Remember, the energy you bring to your relationships determines what you receive in return. When you approach connections with authenticity, kindness, and positivity, you naturally attract people who reflect those qualities back to you.

This New Year, commit to manifesting relationships that align with your highest self and bring out the best in you and others.

**Chapter 9: Harnessing the Energy of New Year's Day**

*Discover the astrological and energetic significance of New Year's Day and how to use it to supercharge your goals.*

**Why New Year's Day Is Energetically Significant**

New Year's Day is a globally recognized turning point, marking the end of one cycle and the beginning of another. While the date itself is based on the Gregorian calendar, its collective celebration infuses it with powerful energetic and psychological momentum. Billions of people focusing on renewal, hope, and fresh starts create a surge of positive energy that you can harness for personal growth and manifestation.

This chapter explores the astrological, symbolic, and energetic importance of New Year's Day and provides actionable steps to tap into its power to supercharge your goals.

**The Symbolism of New Year's Day**

1. **A Blank Slate**: The New Year represents a fresh start, untainted by past mistakes or regrets. It's a chance to recalibrate and align your actions with your higher purpose.
2. **Global Focus**: Collective consciousness amplifies the energy of intention-setting, creating a fertile ground for manifestation.
3. **Rituals of Renewal**: The widespread practice of making resolutions, reflecting on the past year, and envisioning the future imbues the day with transformational energy.

**Astrological Insights for New Year's Day**

Although New Year's Day does not align with traditional astrological cycles, understanding the cosmic backdrop can add depth to your plans.

**1. The Sun in Capricorn**

- **Energy**: Capricorn, ruled by Saturn, embodies discipline, ambition, and structure. The Sun's position in this sign provides a grounded and focused energy, perfect for goal-setting and creating practical plans.
- **How to Harness It**:
  - Prioritize long-term goals that require perseverance.
  - Break down ambitious visions into actionable steps.

**2. Lunar Influence**

The moon phase on New Year's Day varies each year, but it always plays a vital role in shaping the energy of the day.

- **Waxing Moon**: Ideal for building momentum and setting new intentions.
- **Waning Moon**: Perfect for releasing old habits and clearing space for new opportunities.
- **New Moon**: Amplifies fresh starts and creative energy.
- **Full Moon**: Enhances clarity, celebration, and emotional alignment.

**3. Numerological Energy**

- The number of the year (e.g., 2024 adds up to 8) holds unique vibrations. In numerology, 8 symbolizes abundance, balance, and power, which can guide your intentions for the year.
- **How to Use It**: Reflect on the year's numerological meaning to inspire your goals and affirmations.

### Harnessing the Collective Energy of New Year's Day

Billions of people celebrating renewal simultaneously create a powerful energetic wave. Tuning into this collective focus enhances your ability to manifest.

**Steps to Harness Collective Energy:**

1. **Meditate at Midnight**: As the clock strikes midnight, sit in quiet reflection. Visualize yourself connecting with the global wave of hope and possibility.
2. **Set Intentions in Sync**: Align your goals with the collective focus on health, success, and joy. The shared energy amplifies your intentions.
3. **Gratitude Practice**: Start the day with gratitude for the opportunity to begin anew, tuning into the positive momentum of others.

**Preparing for New Year's Day**

**1. Reflect on the Past Year**

Take time to review the previous year to identify lessons, accomplishments, and areas for growth.

- **Questions to Ask**:
  - What were my biggest successes, and what did they teach me?
  - What challenges did I face, and how did I grow from them?
  - What patterns or habits am I ready to release?

**2. Clear Your Space**

Physical and energetic clutter can block new opportunities. Decluttering before New Year's Day creates a clean slate for fresh energy.

- **Action Steps**:
  - Clean your home, focusing on spaces you use frequently.
  - Smudge your space with sage or palo santo to clear stagnant energy.
  - Donate or discard items that no longer serve you.

**3. Craft Your Vision**

Create a vision for the year ahead that reflects your aspirations, values, and desires.

- Use tools like a vision board, journal, or digital planner to map out your goals.
- Include images, affirmations, and keywords that evoke the energy you want to embody.

### New Year's Day Rituals to Supercharge Your Goals

### 1. Morning Intention-Setting Ceremony

Begin the day with a focused intention-setting practice to align your energy with your goals.

**Steps**:

1. **Create a Sacred Space**: Light candles, burn incense, or play calming music to set the mood.
2. **Meditate on Your Goals**: Close your eyes and visualize your ideal year. Imagine each goal as if it's already achieved.
3. **Write Down Intentions**: Use present-tense statements like, "I am thriving in my career and attracting abundance effortlessly."
4. **Seal Your Intentions**: Hold your written intentions and say them aloud, affirming your commitment.

### 2. Prosperity Ritual

Invoke abundance and financial success for the year ahead.

**Steps**:

1. **Prepare Symbolic Items**: Gather coins, green candles, and herbs like basil or cinnamon (associated with wealth).
2. **Light the Candle**: Focus on its flame as a symbol of your financial goals coming to life.
3. **Visualize Abundance**: Picture money flowing into your life and opportunities opening up.
4. **Place the Coins**: Scatter the coins in your home, especially near entryways, to invite prosperity.

### 3. Release and Renew Ritual

Let go of the past to make room for new energy.

**Steps**:

1. **Write It Down**: List everything you want to release from the previous year (e.g., limiting beliefs, bad habits, unresolved emotions).
2. **Burn or Tear the List**: Safely burn or tear up the paper, symbolizing release.
3. **Replace with Positivity**: Write a new list of empowering habits, beliefs, and goals for the year ahead.

### 4. Affirmation Writing

Affirmations help reprogram your subconscious mind to align with your goals.

**Examples**:

- "I am worthy of achieving my dreams."
- "This year, I attract success, love, and abundance effortlessly."
- "Every day, I grow closer to my highest potential."

**Integrating New Year's Energy into Your Year**

Harnessing the energy of New Year's Day doesn't end after January 1st. Use it as a foundation to maintain focus and momentum throughout the year.

**Tips for Sustained Alignment:**

1. **Create Monthly Check-Ins**: Review your goals and intentions at the start of each month. Reflect on progress and make adjustments.
2. **Celebrate Small Wins**: Acknowledge every step forward, no matter how small. Gratitude keeps you motivated.
3. **Stay Flexible**: Life is unpredictable. Be willing to adapt your goals to align with new opportunities or challenges.
4. **Reconnect with Rituals**: Repeat New Year's rituals during significant moments, such as the start of a new season or lunar phase.

**Final Thoughts**

New Year's Day is more than just a date on the calendar—it's a powerful opportunity to align your energy, intentions, and actions with the life you want to create. By understanding its astrological and energetic significance and incorporating meaningful rituals, you can supercharge your goals and set the tone for a transformative year.

This year, make New Year's Day a sacred space to reflect, dream, and take the first steps toward your brightest future. The energy is yours to harness—use it wisely and watch your dreams unfold.

**Chapter 10: Celebrating Your Growth**

*Reflect on milestones, celebrate small wins, and keep the momentum going throughout the year.*

**Why Celebrating Growth Matters**

Celebration is more than just recognizing achievements; it's an essential part of personal development. When you celebrate your growth, you affirm your progress, build confidence, and reinforce positive habits. This acknowledgment creates a feedback loop, motivating you to stay on track and pursue your goals with renewed energy.

Growth isn't just about reaching big milestones. It's also about the small, everyday victories that make those milestones possible. By learning to celebrate both, you cultivate a mindset of gratitude and resilience that propels you forward throughout the year.

**The Psychology of Celebrating Success**

Celebrating growth triggers positive emotions that strengthen your commitment to long-term goals. Here's why it works:

1. **Boosts Motivation**: Recognizing achievements releases dopamine, a "feel-good" chemical that reinforces productive behavior.
2. **Builds Confidence**: Celebrating small wins reminds you of your capabilities, empowering you to take on bigger challenges.
3. **Shifts Your Focus**: Instead of fixating on what you haven't done, celebrating redirects your attention to how far you've come.
4. **Creates Positive Habits**: Regular celebration helps establish a mindset of gratitude and achievement, fostering sustainable growth.

**Step 1: Reflecting on Your Growth**

Reflection is a powerful tool for self-awareness and personal development. By taking time to look back on your journey, you gain clarity about your progress, strengths, and areas for improvement.

**How to Reflect on Milestones:**

1. **Set Time for Reflection**: Choose a consistent schedule—monthly, quarterly, or at the end of major projects—to review your progress.
2. **Ask Reflective Questions**:
   - What were my key achievements this month/year?
   - What challenges did I overcome, and how did they shape me?
   - How have I grown emotionally, mentally, or spiritually?
   - What am I most proud of?
3. **Journal Your Reflections**: Writing down your thoughts allows you to track your growth over time and revisit moments of pride and learning.

**Tools for Tracking Progress:**

- **Goal-Tracking Apps**: Use digital tools like Trello, Notion, or habit trackers to monitor milestones.
- **Vision Board Updates**: Revisit and adjust your vision board to reflect achieved goals and new aspirations.
- **Gratitude Journal**: Dedicate a section to noting accomplishments, both big and small.

**Step 2: Celebrating Small Wins**

Small wins are the building blocks of major achievements. Acknowledging these incremental successes keeps you motivated and focused.

**Why Small Wins Matter:**

- They provide immediate gratification, reinforcing positive behavior.
- They break large goals into manageable, rewarding steps.
- They remind you that progress is a journey, not a destination.

**How to Celebrate Small Wins:**

1. **Create a Rewards System:**
   - Assign a small reward for every step completed toward a larger goal. For example, treat yourself to a favorite snack, movie night, or time off.
2. **Acknowledge Effort, Not Just Results:**
   - Celebrate the effort you put into challenging tasks, even if the outcome isn't perfect.
3. **Share Your Wins:**
   - Tell a friend, family member, or accountability partner about your progress. Sharing creates a sense of community and support.
4. **Mark Your Calendar:**
   - Highlight small victories on your planner or calendar to visualize how consistently you're progressing.
5. **Affirm Yourself:**
   - Use affirmations to recognize your growth, such as, "I am proud of the progress I've made today."

## Step 3: Celebrating Major Milestones

When you reach a significant goal, take time to fully honor your achievement. Celebrating major milestones not only validates your hard work but also strengthens your belief in your ability to achieve even greater goals.

**Ways to Celebrate Major Achievements:**

1. **Plan a Personal Ceremony**:
   - Create a meaningful ritual, such as lighting a candle, writing a letter to yourself, or meditating on your success.
2. **Throw a Celebration**:
   - Host a gathering with friends or family to share your accomplishment. Whether it's a dinner, party, or virtual hangout, celebrating with others amplifies joy.
3. **Document Your Journey**:
   - Capture your milestone through photos, videos, or a journal entry. Revisiting these moments can inspire you in the future.
4. **Invest in Yourself**:
   - Use a portion of your reward to invest in personal growth, such as enrolling in a course, purchasing a new tool, or taking a trip that rejuvenates you.
5. **Pay It Forward**:
   - Celebrate your success by giving back. Volunteer, mentor someone, or donate to a cause that resonates with you.

**Step 4: Creating Rituals of Celebration**

Celebration rituals transform your achievements into meaningful moments of gratitude and joy. These rituals can be simple or elaborate, depending on what feels right for you.

**Examples of Celebration Rituals:**

1. **Gratitude Letter**: Write a letter of gratitude to yourself, high-lighting your hard work and perseverance.
2. **Symbolic Gesture**: Plant a tree, light a candle, or place a mean-ingful object in your home as a reminder of your accomplishment.
3. **Self-Care Day**: Dedicate a day to relaxing, recharging, and pampering yourself.
4. **Creative Expression**: Celebrate through art, music, or writing. Create something that symbolizes your growth.

**Step 5: Maintaining Momentum**

Celebration isn't just about looking back; it's also about fueling your journey forward. After celebrating a win, focus on maintaining momentum and setting new intentions.

**How to Keep the Momentum Going:**

1. **Reflect and Adjust**:
   - After each milestone, evaluate what worked well and what can be improved. Use these insights to refine your next steps.
2. **Set the Next Goal**:
   - Build on your success by identifying a new challenge or aspiration. Break it into actionable steps, just as you did before.
3. **Stay Consistent**:
   - Continue daily habits and rituals that contributed to your growth. Consistency is the key to long-term success.
4. **Stay Inspired**:
   - Surround yourself with motivation, whether it's books, podcasts, or mentors who encourage you to keep pushing forward.
5. **Celebrate Along the Way**:
   - Don't wait until the end to celebrate. Acknowledge progress at every stage to stay energized and positive.

**Step 6: Embracing Gratitude for the Journey**

Gratitude is the ultimate form of celebration. It shifts your focus from what's missing to what you've gained, creating a sense of abundance and fulfillment.

**Daily Gratitude Practices:**

- Write down three things you're grateful for each evening.
- Reflect on the people, experiences, and lessons that have supported your growth.
- Practice gratitude for challenges, recognizing how they've shaped your resilience and strength.

**Success Stories: The Power of Celebration**

1. **The Entrepreneur's Growth:**
   - A small business owner celebrated every sale, no matter how small, by writing a thank-you note to her customers. This practice kept her motivated and helped her business grow exponentially over the year.

2. **The Weight-Loss Journey:**
   - A woman set mini rewards for each milestone in her weight-loss journey, like buying a new outfit or trying a new activity. Celebrating along the way kept her focused and made the process enjoyable.

3. **The Aspiring Writer:**
   - An aspiring author celebrated finishing each chapter of their book with a favorite treat. This simple ritual made the daunting task of writing a full manuscript feel manageable and rewarding.

### Final Thoughts

Celebrating your growth is a powerful way to honor your journey, build confidence, and sustain your momentum. By reflecting on milestones, recognizing small wins, and embracing gratitude, you transform your goals from tasks into meaningful experiences.

Remember, every step forward—no matter how small—is a step closer to becoming the person you aspire to be. Celebrate often, celebrate fully, and let the joy of your progress propel you into an even brighter future.

### Appendix A: Tools for Manifestation Success

*A curated list of recommended crystals, herbs, and tools to amplify your New Year's rituals.*

### Why Use Tools for Manifestation?

Manifestation tools are physical and symbolic items that help you focus your energy, enhance your rituals, and strengthen your intentions. These tools work by amplifying your vibrational alignment with the goals you wish to achieve. Whether you're setting New Year's resolutions, creating a vision board, or performing a prosperity ritual, incorporating these tools can deepen your practice and increase its effectiveness.

### Recommended Crystals for Manifestation

Crystals are natural amplifiers of energy, each carrying unique properties that can support your manifestation goals. Below is a list of crystals and their uses:

### 1. Clear Quartz (The Master Manifestor)

- **Properties**: Amplifies energy, clears negativity, and enhances focus.
- **How to Use**: Hold while setting intentions or place on your vision board to amplify your goals.

### 2. Citrine (The Stone of Abundance)

- **Properties**: Attracts wealth, success, and positivity; boosts confidence.
- **How to Use**: Keep in your wallet to attract financial abundance or place on your altar during prosperity rituals.

## 3. Amethyst (The Stone of Intuition)

- **Properties**: Enhances clarity, spiritual connection, and inner peace.
- **How to Use**: Meditate with amethyst to gain insight into your goals or place near your bed for restful sleep and clarity of mind.

## 4. Green Aventurine (The Stone of Opportunity)

- **Properties**: Brings luck, growth, and new opportunities.
- **How to Use**: Carry in your pocket during job interviews, meetings, or other important events.

## 5. Pyrite (Fool's Gold)

- **Properties**: Attracts prosperity, protects against negative energy, and boosts motivation.
- **How to Use**: Place on your desk to attract career success or use in money jar spells.

## 6. Rose Quartz (The Stone of Love)

- **Properties**: Promotes self-love, compassion, and harmony in relationships.
- **How to Use**: Use in rituals to manifest healthy relationships or keep in your space to invite loving energy.

### 7. Carnelian (The Stone of Motivation)

- **Properties**: Ignites creativity, boosts courage, and strengthens determination.
- **How to Use**: Hold during goal-setting sessions or place near your workspace to enhance productivity.

### 8. Selenite (The Cleansing Crystal)

- **Properties**: Clears energy, promotes mental clarity, and aligns intentions with higher vibrations.
- **How to Use**: Use to cleanse your tools and space before rituals or meditation.

### Recommended Herbs for Manifestation

Herbs carry powerful energies that can enhance your manifestation practice. They can be burned, infused into oils, added to baths, or used in spells.

### 1. Basil

- **Properties**: Attracts prosperity, clears negativity, and promotes harmony.
- **How to Use**: Sprinkle dried basil around your workspace for financial success or add fresh basil to your food with the intention of abundance.

### 2. Cinnamon

- **Properties**: Boosts energy, accelerates manifestations, and attracts wealth.
- **How to Use**: Burn cinnamon sticks for prosperity rituals or sprinkle powdered cinnamon into a money jar spell.

### 3. Lavender

- **Properties**: Promotes peace, relaxation, and clarity.
- **How to Use**: Use in bath rituals to clear your mind before setting intentions or burn lavender to calm energy during meditation.

### 4. Bay Leaves

- **Properties**: Enhances wish fulfillment and brings good luck.
- **How to Use**: Write your intentions on a bay leaf and burn it to release your wishes into the universe.

### 5. Sage

- **Properties**: Clears negative energy and creates a sacred space.
- **How to Use**: Burn sage to cleanse your space and tools before performing rituals.

### 6. Rosemary

- **Properties**: Encourages clarity, protection, and personal power.
- **How to Use**: Add rosemary to candles or oils used in rituals for focus and determination.

### 7. Mint

- **Properties**: Attracts wealth, clears mental fog, and invigorates energy.
- **How to Use**: Place fresh mint leaves in your wallet or purse to attract financial growth.

### 8. Chamomile

- **Properties**: Promotes calm, success, and abundance.
- **How to Use**: Brew into tea to relax and focus your energy before manifestation practices.

## Recommended Tools for Manifestation

In addition to crystals and herbs, various tools can enhance your manifestation rituals.

### 1. Candles

- **Purpose**: Symbolize transformation and amplify intentions.
- **How to Use**:
    - **Color Correspondence**:
        - Green for abundance and growth.
        - White for clarity and purity.
        - Yellow for confidence and creativity.
    - Carve your intention into the candle and light it during rituals.

### 2. Journals

- **Purpose**: Capture intentions, reflect on progress, and record manifestations.
- **How to Use**:
    - Write affirmations daily.
    - Use scripting to describe your goals as if they've already been achieved.

### 3. Vision Boards

- **Purpose**: Visualize your goals and maintain focus.
- **How to Use**: Include images, affirmations, and symbols that align with your desires. Place the board in a location you'll see daily.

### 4. Singing Bowls or Sound Tools

- **Purpose**: Raise vibrations and clear stagnant energy.
- **How to Use**: Use sound to cleanse your space or enhance meditation sessions.

### 5. Essential Oils

- **Purpose**: Enhance rituals with aromatherapy.
- **How to Use**:
    - Diffuse oils like frankincense for spiritual alignment or orange for joy and prosperity.
    - Apply diluted oils to your pulse points with intention.

### 6. Altar or Sacred Space

- **Purpose**: Provide a dedicated area for rituals and reflection.
- **How to Use**: Decorate with crystals, herbs, candles, and meaningful objects that resonate with your goals.

### 7. Pendulum

- **Purpose**: Gain clarity and confirm decisions.
- **How to Use**: Ask yes/no questions to help align your actions with your intentions.

### 8. Mirrors

- **Purpose**: Reflect and amplify energy.
- **How to Use**: Perform affirmations in front of a mirror to strengthen self-belief and focus.

## Combining Tools for Maximum Effect

The most effective manifestation practices integrate multiple tools to create a synergistic effect.

### Example Ritual: Prosperity Manifestation

1. **Preparation**: Cleanse your space with sage or selenite.
2. **Set the Mood**: Light a green candle and diffuse basil or cinnamon essential oil.
3. **Create the Spell**: Write your financial goal on a bay leaf. Place it in a jar with citrine, pyrite, and mint leaves.
4. **Affirm**: Speak an affirmation aloud, such as, "I attract wealth and abundance effortlessly."
5. **Close the Ritual**: Meditate with your jar or place it on your altar.

## Final Thoughts

Manifestation tools serve as powerful aids in focusing your energy and aligning your actions with your intentions. By incorporating crystals, herbs, and other tools into your New Year's rituals, you amplify your ability to attract the life you desire.

Experiment with the tools that resonate most with you, and remember that your intention is the most potent force of all. When you combine belief, action, and the support of these tools, your manifestations become not only possible but inevitable.

**Appendix B: Journal Prompts for a Magical Year**

*Guided prompts to help you deepen your self-reflection and track your progress throughout the year.*

**Why Journaling Is Essential for a Magical Year**

Journaling is a powerful tool for self-reflection, intention setting, and tracking your personal growth. By putting your thoughts and feelings into words, you clarify your goals, deepen your connection with yourself, and create a tangible record of your journey. Journaling transforms abstract ideas into actionable insights, helping you stay aligned with your intentions throughout the year.

This appendix provides guided prompts tailored to different aspects of your life, allowing you to reflect on your progress, celebrate your successes, and adjust your course as needed.

**Getting Started with Journaling**

Before diving into the prompts, set the stage for a meaningful journaling practice:

1. **Create a Sacred Space**: Find a quiet and comfortable spot where you can write without distractions. Light a candle, burn incense, or play calming music to set the mood.
2. **Choose Your Tools**: Use a journal that inspires you—whether it's a beautifully bound notebook, a digital app, or a simple pad of paper.
3. **Set an Intention**: Before each journaling session, take a deep breath and reflect on what you want to gain from the practice (e.g., clarity, gratitude, insight).
4. **Write Freely**: Let your thoughts flow without judgment. There's no right or wrong way to journal.

**Prompts for New Beginnings**

Start your year with clarity and purpose by reflecting on your desires, values, and goals.

1. **What do I want to leave behind from the past year? What lessons have I learned that I can carry forward?**
2. **If I could create my dream life, what would it look like? What specific elements bring me joy, fulfillment, and peace?**
3. **What are my top three priorities for this year? How can I align my actions with these priorities?**
4. **What limiting beliefs do I need to release to step into my highest potential?**
5. **What does success mean to me? How will I know when I've achieved it?**

**Prompts for Setting Intentions**

These prompts will help you clarify your goals and create intentions that resonate with your values.

1. **What is one area of my life I want to transform this year? Why is this important to me?**
2. **What specific actions can I take this month to move closer to my goals?**
3. **What qualities or habits do I want to cultivate in myself? How can I incorporate them into my daily life?**
4. **What are three affirmations I can use to stay focused and motivated?**
5. **How can I ensure my goals align with my personal values and long-term vision?**

**Prompts for Monthly Reflections**

Use these prompts at the end of each month to assess your progress and adjust your course.

1. **What were my biggest achievements this month? How did they make me feel?**
2. **What challenges did I face, and what lessons did I learn from them?**
3. **What actions brought me closer to my goals? What could I improve on next month?**
4. **How did I take care of my mind, body, and spirit this month?**
5. **What am I most grateful for right now, and why?**

**Prompts for Overcoming Obstacles**

When you encounter challenges, these prompts can help you gain perspective and find solutions.

1. **What is the current obstacle I'm facing, and how does it make me feel?**
2. **What strengths or resources do I have that can help me overcome this challenge?**
3. **What is one small step I can take today to move forward?**
4. **How has this challenge helped me grow or shift my perspective?**
5. **What support do I need, and how can I ask for it?**

**Prompts for Celebrating Growth**

Regularly celebrating your progress keeps you motivated and aligned with your goals.

1. What is one small win I achieved today/this week? How can I celebrate it?
2. How have I grown emotionally, mentally, or spiritually over the past month?
3. What qualities in myself am I most proud of?
4. What are three things I've accomplished this year that I never thought I could?
5. How can I express gratitude to myself and others for supporting my journey?

**Prompts for Gratitude and Mindfulness**

Gratitude enhances your perspective and helps you stay present in your journey.

1. What are three things I'm grateful for today? How do they make my life better?
2. Who has made a positive impact on my life recently? How can I show appreciation for them?
3. What is one beautiful or inspiring moment I experienced this week?
4. What small joys or blessings do I often overlook?
5. How can I bring more gratitude and mindfulness into my daily routine?

**Prompts for Long-Term Visioning**

These prompts encourage you to dream big and create a roadmap for your future.

1. **Where do I see myself in one year? Five years? Ten years?**
2. **What legacy do I want to leave behind? How can I start building it today?**
3. **If I knew I couldn't fail, what would I pursue, and why?**
4. **What does living my best life look and feel like?**
5. **What steps can I take now to align my present actions with my long-term vision?**

**Prompts for Seasonal Alignment**

Reflecting on seasonal cycles connects you with nature and helps you flow with its rhythms.

**Spring:**

- What seeds of intention am I planting this season?
- How can I embrace growth and renewal in my life?

**Summer:**

- What successes am I celebrating this season?
- How can I maintain balance while enjoying the energy of expansion?

**Autumn:**

- What am I harvesting from my efforts this year?
- What habits or patterns am I ready to release as the year winds down?

**Winter:**

- How can I use this time for rest and reflection?
- What goals or intentions am I preparing to focus on in the coming year?

**Prompts for Manifestation**

These prompts help you refine your manifestation practice and align with your desires.

1. **What do I want to manifest in my life right now? Why is this important to me?**
2. **What beliefs or habits might be blocking my manifestations?**
3. **How can I align my daily actions with the energy of abundance and success?**
4. **What does my dream life feel like, and how can I embody that feeling today?**
5. **What signs or synchronicities have I noticed that confirm I'm on the right path?**

**How to Use These Prompts Throughout the Year**

1. **Daily Practice**: Select one prompt each morning or evening to reflect on.
2. **Monthly Themes**: Dedicate a month to exploring a specific area, such as gratitude, goal setting, or seasonal alignment.
3. **Ritual Integration**: Incorporate journaling into your manifestation or meditation rituals to deepen your practice.
4. **Review Progress**: Revisit your journal entries regularly to track your growth and gain new insights.

**Final Thoughts**

Journaling is one of the most powerful tools for creating a magical and transformative year. By engaging with these prompts, you'll deepen your self-awareness, strengthen your intentions, and stay aligned with your goals.

Let your journal become a trusted companion on your journey, guiding you through challenges, celebrating your victories, and helping you manifest the life you've always envisioned. The magic is in the process—so write, reflect, and watch your dreams unfold.

## Message from the Author:

I hope you enjoyed this book, I love astrology and knew there was not a book such as this out on the shelf. I love metaphysical items as well. Please check out my other books:

-Life of Government Benefits

-My life of Hell

-My life with Hydrocephalus

-Red Sky

-World Domination:Woman's rule

-World Domination:Woman's Rule 2: The War

-Life and Banishment of Apophis: book 1

-The Kidney Friendly Diet

-The Ultimate Hemp Cookbook

-Creating a Dispensary(legally)

-Cleanliness throughout life: the importance of showering from childhood to adulthood.

-Strong Roots: The Risks of Overcoddling children

-Hemp Horoscopes: Cosmic Insights and Earthly Healing

- Celestial Hemp Navigating the Zodiac: Through the Green Cosmos

-Astrological Hemp: Aligning The Stars with Earth's Ancient Herb

-The Astrological Guide to Hemp: Stars, Signs, and Sacred Leaves

-Green Growth: Innovative Marketing Strategies for your Hemp Products and Dispensary

-Cosmic Cannabis

-Astrological Munchies

-Henry The Hemp

-Zodiacal Roots: The Astrological Soul Of Hemp

**- Green Constellations: Intersection of Hemp and Zodiac**

-Hemp in The Houses: An astrological Adventure Through The Cannabis Galaxy

-Galactic Ganja Guide

Heavenly Hemp

Zodiac Leaves

Doctor Who Astrology

Cannastrology

Stellar Satvias and Cosmic Indicas

<u>Celestial Cannabis: A Zodiac Journey</u>

AstroHerbology: The Sky and The Soil: Volume 1

AstroHerbology:Celestial Cannabis:Volume 2

Cosmic Cannabis Cultivation

The Starry Guide to Herbal Harmony: Volume 1

The Starry Guide to Herbal Harmony: Cannabis Universe: Volume 2

Yugioh Astrology: Astrological Guide to Deck, Duels and more

Nightmare Mansion: Echoes of The Abyss

**Nightmare Mansion 2: Legacy of Shadows**

**Nightmare Mansion 3: Shadows of the Forgotten**

Nightmare Mansion 4: Echoes of the Damned

The Life and Banishment of Apophis: Book 2

Nightmare Mansion: Halls of Despair

<u>Healing with Herb: Cannabis and Hydrocephalus</u>

**<u>Planetary Pot: Aligning with Astrological Herbs: Volume 1</u>**

**Fast Track to Freedom: 30 Days to Financial Independence Using AI, Assets, and Agile Hustles**

**<u>Cosmic Hemp Pathways</u>**

**How to Become Financially Free in 30 Days: 10,000 Paths to Prosperity**

**Zodiacal Herbage: Astrological Insights: Volume 1**

Nightmare Mansion: Whispers in the Walls

The Daleks Invade Atlantis

**Henry the hemp and Hydrocephalus**

10X The Kidney Friendly Diet

Cannabis Universe: Adult coloring book

**Hemp Astrology: The Healing Power of the Stars**

**Zodiacal Herbage: Astrological Insights: Cannabis Universe: Volume 2**

**<u>Planetary Pot: Aligning with Astrological Herbs: Cannabis Universes: Volume 2</u>**

Doctor Who Meets the Replicators and SG-1: The Ultimate Battle for Survival

Nightmare Mansion: Curse of the Blood Moon

**<u>The Celestial Stoner: A Guide to the Zodiac</u>**

**Cosmic Pleasures: Sex Toy Astrology for Every Sign**

Hydrocephalus Astrology: Navigating the Stars and Healing Waters

**Lapis and the Mischievous Chocolate Bar**

Celestial Positions: Sexual Astrology for Every Sign

Apophis's Shadow Work Journal: : A Journey of Self-Discovery and Healing

**Kinky Cosmos: Sexual Kink Astrology for Every Sign**

**Digital Cosmos: The Astrological Digimon Compendium**

**Stellar Seeds: The Cosmic Guide to Growing with Astrology**

Apophis's Daily Gratitude Journal

Cat Astrology: Feline Mysteries of the Cosmos

**The Cosmic Kama Sutra: An Astrological Guide to Sexual Positions**

**Unleash Your Potential: A Guided Journal Powered by AI Insights**

**Whispers of the Enchanted Grove**

Cosmic Pleasures: An Astrological Guide to Sexual Kinks

369, 12 Manifestation Journal

Whisper of the nocturne journal(blank journal for writing or drawing)

The Boogey Book

Locked In Reflection: A Chastity Journey Through Locktober

Generating Wealth Quickly:

How to Generate $100,000 in 24 Hours

Star Magic: Harness the Power of the Universe

The Flatulence Chronicles: A Fart Journal for Self-Discovery

The Doctor and The Death Moth

Seize the Day: A Personal Seizure Tracking Journal

The Ultimate Boogeyman Safari: A Journey into the Boogie World and Beyond

**Whispers of Samhain: 1,000 Spells of Love, Luck, and Lunar Magic: Samhain Spell Book**

**Apophis's guides:**

**Witch's Spellbook Crafting Guide for Halloween**

<u>**Frost & Flame: The Enchanted Yule Grimoire of 1000 Winter Spells**</u>

<u>**The Ultimate Boogey Goo Guide & Spooky Activities for Halloween Fun**</u>

Harmony of the Scales: A Libra's Spellcraft for Balance and Beauty

The Enchanted Advent: 36 Days of Christmas Wonders

**Nightmare Mansion: The Labyrinth of Screams**

Harvest of Enchantment: 1,000 Spells of Gratitude, Love, and Fortune for Thanksgiving

The Boogey Chronicles: A Journal of Nightly Encounters and Shadowy Secrets

The 12 Days of Financial Freedom: A Step-by-Step Christmas Countdown to Transform Your Finances

Sigil of the Eternal Spiral Blank Journal

A Christmas Feast: Timeless Recipes for Every Meal

Holiday Stress-Free Solutions: A Survival Guide to Thriving During the Festive Season

Yu-Gi-Oh! Holiday Gifting Mastery: The Ultimate Guide for Fans and Newcomers Alike

Holiday Harmony: A Hydrocephalus Survival Guide for the Festive Season

Celestial Craft: The Witch's Almanac for 2025 – A Cosmic Guide to Manifestations, Moons, and Mystical Events

Doctor Who: The Toymaker's Winter Wonderland

Tulsa King Unveiled: A Thrilling Guide to Stallone's Mafia Masterpiece

Pendulum Craft: A Complete Guide to Crafting and Using Personalized Divination Tools

Nightmare Mansion: Santa's Eternal Eve

Starlight Noel: A Cosmic Journey through Christmas Mysteries

The Dark Architect: Unlocking the Blueprint of Existence

Surviving the Embrace: The Ultimate Guide to Encounters with The Hugging Molly

The Enchanted Codex: Secrets of the Craft for Witches, Wiccans, and Pagans

Harvest of Gratitude: A Complete Thanksgiving Guide

Yuletide Essentials: A Complete Guide to an Authentic and Magical Christmas

Celestial Smokes: A Cosmic Guide to Cigars and Astrology

Living in Balance: A Comprehensive Survival Guide to Thriving with Diabetes Insipidus

Cosmic Symbiosis: The Venom Zodiac Chronicles

*The Cursed Paw of Ambition*

Cosmic Symbiosis: The Astrological Venom Journal

Celestial Wonders Unfold: A Stargazer's Guide to the Cosmos (2024-2029)

The Ultimate Black Friday Prepper's Guide: Mastering Shopping Strategies and Savings

*Cosmic Sales: The Astrological Guide to Black Friday Shopping*

Legends of the Corn Mother and Other Harvest Myths

Whispers of the Harvest: The Corn Mother's Journal

The Evergreen Spellbook

The Doctor Meets the Boogeyman

The White Witch of Rose Hall's SpellBook

**The Gingerbread Golem's Shadow: A Study in Sweet Darkness**

**The Gingerbread Golem Codex: An Academic Exploration of Sweet Myths**

The Gingerbread Golem Grimoire: Sweet Magicks and Spells for the Festive Witch

**The Curse of the Gingerbread Golem**

10-minute Christmas Crafts for kids

**<u>Christmas Crisis Solutions: The Ultimate Last-Minute Survival Guide</u>**

Gingerbread Golem Recipes: Holiday Treats with a Magical Twist

*The Infinite Key: Unlocking Mystical Secrets of the Ages*

Enchanted Yule: A Wiccan and Pagan Guide to a Magical and Memorable Season

Dinosaurs of Power: Unlocking Ancient Magick

Astro-Dinos: The Cosmic Guide to Prehistoric Wisdom

Gallifrey's Yule Logs: A Festive Doctor Who Cookbook

**The Dino Grimoire: Secrets of Prehistoric Magick**

**The Gift They Never Knew They Needed**

*The Gingerbread Golem's Culinary Alchemy: Enchanting Recipes for a Sweetly Dark Feast*

A Time Lord Christmas: Holiday Adventures with the Doctor

**Krampusproofing Your Home: Defensive Strategies for Yule**

Silent Frights: A Collection of Christmas Creepypastas to Chill Your Bones

***Santa Raptor's Jolly Carnage: A Dino-Claus Christmas Tale***

Prehistoric Palettes: A Dino Wicca Coloring Journey

The Christmas Wishkeeper Chronicles

The Starlight Sleigh: A Holiday Journey

***Elf Secrets: The True Magic of the North Pole***

Candy Cane Conjurations

***Cooking with Kids: Recipes Under 20 Minutes***

Doctor Who: The TARDIS Confiscation

*The Anxiety First Aid Kit: Quick Tools to Calm Your Mind*

Frosty Whispers: A Winter's Tale

The Infinite Key: Unlocking the Secrets to Prosperity, Resilience, and Purpose

The Grasping Void: Why You'll Regret This Purchase

Astrology for Busy Bees: Star Signs Simplified

***The Instant Focus Formula: Cut Through the Noise***

The Secret Language of Colors: Unlocking the Emotional Codes

Sacred Fossil Chronicles: Blank Journal

**The Christmas Cottage Miracle**

**Feeding Frenzy: Graboid-Inspired Recipes**

**Manifest in Minutes: The Quick Law of Attraction Guide**

**The Symbiote Chronicles: Doctor Who's Venomous Journey**

**Think Tiny, Grow Big: The Minimalist Mindset**

**The Energy Key: Unlocking Limitless Motivation**

If you want solar for your home go here: https://www.harborsolar.live/apophisenterprises/

Get Some Tarot cards: https://www.makeplayingcards.com/sell/
apophis-occult-shop

<u>**Get some shirts: https://www.bonfire.com/store/apophis-shirt-emporium/**</u>

**Instagrams:**
@apophis_enterprises,
@apophisbookemporium,
@apophisscardshop
Twitter: @apophisenterpr1
 Tiktok:@apophisenterprise
Youtube: @sg1fan23477, @FiresideRetreatKingdom
Hive: @sg1fan23477
CheeLee: @SG1fan23477

**Podcast: Apophis  Chat  Zone:** https://open.spotify.com/show/ 5zXbrCLEV2xzCp8ybrfHsk?si=fb4d4fdbdce44dec

**Newsletter:** https://apophiss-newsletter-27c897.beehiiv.com/

If you want to support me or see posts of other projects that I have come over to: **<u>buymeacoffee.com/mpetchinskg</u>**
I post there daily several times a day

Get your Dinowicca or Christmas themed digital products, especially Santa Raptor songs and other musics. Here: **https://sg1fan23477.gumroad.com**

Apophis Yuletide Digital has not only digital Christmas items, but it will have all things with Dinowicca as well as other Digital products.